AF322673

Splat! Brandon's Big Fit

DEDICATION PAGE

With inexplicable love and gratitude for…

Marsha & Allen Houchins. You always let me write, roam, and find my way. Even when it was the hard way. Thank you for reading to us as kids and instilling my love of storytelling.

Brandon Lee. From colleague to dear friend, your inspiration and encouragement fill my soul. My own healing would not have happened without you. Your heart is as big as your talent and your vulnerability as impressive as your achievements. I'm honored to help tell your story.

Mary Richardson. You have changed my life and relationship with myself and others. Thank you for guiding me to a life of love, compassion, gratitude, joy, and for bravely leading by example.

All the children and adult inner children whose innocence has been stolen, or confidence kicked by bullies of any kind and at any age. You belong. You are enough.

Brandon is sad, mad and acting bad. Bullied at school, he's having trouble coping with some unkind classmates. When his creative and compassionate teacher Miss Wigglesworth steps in, she shows him a fun way to overcome his outbursts, face his feelings and take the first step toward self-acceptance.

Inspired by the real-life childhood of Brandon Lee, former news anchor and best-selling author of "Mascara Boy." Brandon overcame his own painful past and channeled it into his "Art of Our Soul" studio. A place where trauma survivors come to heal by creating beautiful works of acrylic pouring art.

Kicking, screaming, hitting...
Sometimes he'd even spit.
Brandon prided himself on pitching the biggest of fits.

That hole in the wall came from one angry punch!
Simply because he didn't like what was for lunch.

Trashing and smashing things to bits.

Throwing himself on the floor.

Once, Brandon even kicked in a door!

That's when his teacher Miss Wigglesworth said, "No more!"

She kindly sat Brandon down and asked,

"Why are you so mad?"

And you know what he said?

He told her he's actually SAD.

The rage flashing in his eyes, suddenly replaced by tears,
As the boy with beautiful long lashes revealed his fears.

"When I climb on the bus, the insults fly
And all I want to do is cry.
The kids call me 'Mascara Boy' and other cruel names,
Like 'sissy boy' or 'make-up face' and make me feel shame."

"They make fun of my high voice
and long, thick eye-lashes.
I've even tried cutting them in
between classes."

"They taunt me and tease
me and make me feel small,
because I'd rather play with
dress-up dolls, instead of
hitting a ball."

"I see" said Miss Wigglesworth, "that sounds very cruel.

I want you to know there is absolutely

NOTHING WRONG WITH YOU!

But I think there is something we can do."

"We can't control what others do or say
But we can keep it from ruining Our day.
It's okay to be sad, angry, scared or anything else you feel,
But there is a healthier way to deal."

"Let's find you a better emotional outlet.
How 'bout we try turning your tantrums into a talent?
Please meet me after school, in room 23
I have something I think you might like to see."

Brandon was curious, shrugged and nodded his head
"I guess so," he said.

The last school bell shrieked right at 2:30.

All the kids raced to go play and get dirty.

Except Brandon who nervously...

and bravely headed down the hall.

Room 23 ...

Brandon took a big breath then pushed open the door,

without a clue of what was in store.

"Come in, come in" Miss Wigglesworth sang out.
Brandon scanned the room not sure what this was about.
The walls covered in paper, there were canvases too
And gallons of paint in every color and hue.

"When you feel like lashing out, this is the place
you can consider your secret safe space.
You can scream, shout and let your feelings out."

SPLAT!

Miss Wigglesworth took a brush full of orange paint and splattered the wall,
As she let out a primal call.
"See, it feels great!
And instead of destroying, you can create!"

"Now you give it a try" she said handing Brandon the brush.

SPLAT!

Brandon felt a giant rush.

Brandon ran to the table in an excited dash,

Dipped a new brush in yellow and took another pass.

SPLAT!

Next Brandon grabbed a can and started to spray.

Up and down and every which way.

He played and played and played and played.

Suddenly Brandon stopped, admiring the colors covering the walls.

He no longer thought about the names he was called.

Brandon felt good. No wait, he felt great!

Finding this passion was truly fate.

He felt lighter and joyful, his spirits were lifted.
'Mascara Boy' discovered he was truly gifted.

And while it may take time for others to see,
There's also something very special inside you and me.

Miss Wigglesworth's lesson you'll learn before long.

It's not important to fit in...

...because you already belong.